BLESSED QUIETNESS

Sw. Flute Celeste 8'
Gt. Solo reed 8'
Ped. Soft 16' 8'

Upper: 00 4504 002
Lower: 00 8880 000
Pedal: 43

W. S. Marshall
Arranged by John Innes

B-G0693

HOSANNA, LOUD HOSANNA

Sw. Principal chorus and mixtures
Gt. Full, plus mixtures (no reeds)
Ped. 16' 8' Principals, Sw. to Gt.

Upper: 00 5624 224
Lower: 00 6748 446
Pedal: 54

Gesangbuch der Herzogl
Arranged by John Innes

B-G0693

6

B-G0693

O JESUS I HAVE PROMISED

Sw. Oboe 8'
Gt. Soft flute 8'
Ped. Soft 16'

Upper: F# preset
Lower: D# preset or 00 7880 400
Pedal: 54

Arthur H. Mann
Arranged by John Innes

B-G0693

10

B-G0693

ETERNAL FATHER, STRONG TO SAVE

Sw. Full and reeds
Gt. Full, no reeds, Sw. to Gt.
Ped. Full, no reeds, Sw. to Ped.

Upper: 00 5705 002
Lower: 00 7856 045
Pedal: 65

John B. Dykes
Arranged by John Innes

B-G0693

Faster

Swell to Gt. off
Gt. Principal chorus
and mixtures

BLESSED BE THE NAME

Sw. Principal chorus and mixtures
Gt. Full, no reeds Sw. to Gt.
Ped. 16' 8' Principals, Sw. to Ped.

Upper: 00 5707 005
Lower: 00 6747 235
Pedal: 55

Ralph Hudson
Arranged by John Innes

B-G0693

Slightly slower

16' 8' Bourdons (Sw. to Ped. off)
Gt. to Ped.

NEAR TO THE HEART OF GOD

Sw. Flute celeste 8'
Gt. Gedeckt 8'
Ped. Soft 16'

Upper: 00 4505 002
Lower: 00 3414 001
Pedal: 42

Cleland B. McAfee
Arranged by John Innes

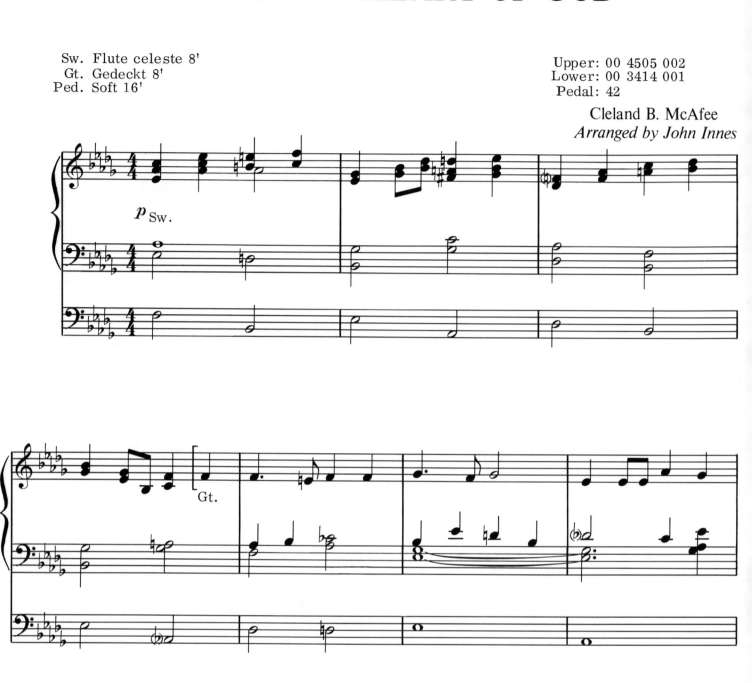

B-G0693

22

B-G 0693

TAKE THE NAME OF JESUS WITH YOU

Sw. Principals 8' 4'
 Gt. Principals 8' 4' 2' Mixt., Sw. to Gt.
Ped. Principals 16' 8' Sw. to Ped.

Upper: 01 7746 224
Lower: 00 7848 335
Pedal: 56

William H. Doane
Arranged by John Innes

Martial tempo

B-G0693

24

B-G0693

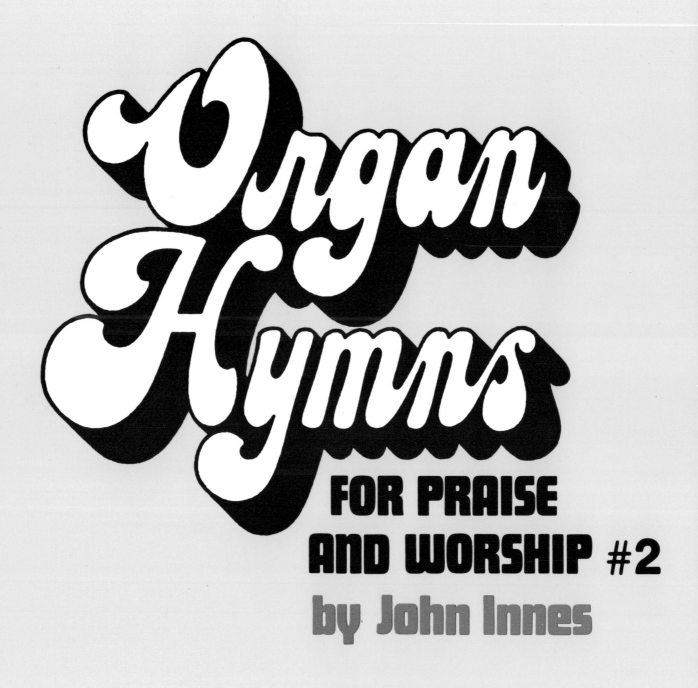

Organ Hymns

FOR PRAISE AND WORSHIP #2
by John Innes

BLESSED BE THE NAME

BLESSED QUIETNESS

ETERNAL FATHER, STRONG TO SAVE

HOSANNA, LOUD HOSANNA

NEAR TO THE HEART OF GOD

O JESUS I HAVE PROMISED

TAKE THE NAME OF JESUS WITH YOU

DISTRIBUTED BY HAL LEONARD

0 73999 38387 4

08738387   U.S. $9.95

HL08738387